Communicating Like a Pro

Professional Pointers for Boosting YOUR Communication Skills

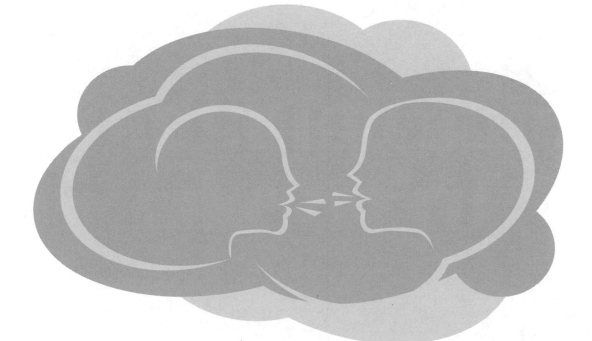

Communicating Like a Pro

*Professional Pointers for Boosting
YOUR Communication Skills*

Deborah Shouse

SkillPath® Publications

Editor: Bill Cowles

Cover design: Jason Sprenger

Layout: Danielle Horn

ISBN: 978-1-934589-11-3

Printed in the United States of America

Acknowledgements

Thanks to Sarah H. Shouse, M.A., Ph.D. Candidate for consulting on this book.

Thanks to my life partner, Ron Zoglin, for his careful reading, editing and excellent suggestions.

Thanks to Barbara Bartocci for her help with the editing process.

Thanks to the many wonderful writers and friends who are a constant source of inspiration and encouragement.

Table of Contents

Chapter One:

Traveling the Tact Track

"That idea really doesn't work for me. Can anyone come up with something better?"
Carol looked around the table.

Tina's throat tightened and her hands clenched. She hated it when Carol criticized her ideas like that. She should have known better than to even speak up in a meeting Carol was in charge of.

Tina wanted to respond but couldn't think of a diplomatic way to translate what she was thinking. She wished she had more diplomatic skills! She wished she knew something brilliant yet tactful to say when she found herself criticized, in a conflict or even in a confusing or tricky situation. She also wished some of her co-workers were more diplomatic and professional in their communication.

For example, just yesterday she walked into yet another meeting and Carol said, too loudly, "Tina, are you all right? You look so tired!"

Tina instantly felt old, ugly and criticized. She imagined big black carry-on bags under her eyes. She also imagined that all six people in the room had stopped to look at her. Finally, she managed to say, "I'm fine, Carol. Thanks for your concern."

After the meeting, she went to the break room to get some coffee. (Maybe she was a little tired, but she certainly didn't want to be told she looked tired!) She overheard someone making a tactless joke about Courtney, the department administrative assistant, and her very eclectic collection of high-heeled and colorful shoes.

The "joke" must have quickly made the rounds, because 30 minutes later Courtney came clomping into Tina's office on some exceedingly high lime-green platforms to get comfort from Tina.

Tina needed some comfort herself that afternoon when she went to report to the Project Team. She had prepared for the meeting. But when two cell phones went off during her presentation, and one of her colleagues actually had a brief, semi-hushed conversation, her confidence dwindled. She stumbled over some of the information and worried she hadn't presented herself professionally.

These days, you don't have to be serving in a foreign embassy or working in community relations to need diplomatic skills. Ordinary business conversations often require a high level of sensitivity and tact. The more you learn about the art of communicating diplomatically and professionally, the more you'll stand out and move ahead in your workplace.

Where Are You on the Tact Track?

Everyone has his or her own communication style. Here are a few examples:

- "I don't believe in beating around the bush," Carol says. "I think if you have something to say you should just say it."
- "I think it all depends on who you're talking to," Kevin believes. "Some people like straight talk, and others can't take it."
- "I like to ease into difficult topics, you know, give people some hints, let them know I have something touchy to discuss," says Stefanie. "If you're too blunt, people may get defensive and aggressive."

Where does your natural tact take you? Are you plowing through, tiptoeing around or taking the temperature of the room? Answer these questions for yourself.

1. Typically, when I have something difficult to say to someone:

   A. I march right up and say what is on my mind as soon as possible.

   B. I give them a hint or two, letting them know I'm upset.

   C. I wait a while, trying to figure out the best way to present the information.

   D. Other

2. When I have an opinion on a subject:

   A. I like to state it clearly.

   B. I wait to see if someone else brings up the same idea.

   C. I listen to other ideas for a while, and try to analyze the mood of the room. That way, I can state my opinion so other people can really hear it.

   D. Other

3. When I'm preparing a presentation:

   A. I try to put as much of my personality into the talk as possible.

   B. I try to keep my personality out and concentrate on the topic at hand.

   C. I learn about the audience and add stories that they might relate to.

   D. Other

4. When I find myself in the middle of an argument or a conflict situation:

   A. I try to keep my ideas at the forefront of the conversation.

   B. I back way down and become as invisible as possible.

   C. I ask questions, so I can learn where the commonalities are.

   D. Other

5. When I'm in a social situation:

   A. I try to introduce myself to as many people as possible. I enjoy networking.

   B. I find people I already know and hang out with them.

   C. I try to get into interesting conversations and I try to include as many people as possible.

   D. Other

If you've chosen a lot of A's, you have a gift for direct communication. You're not afraid to notice what's going on and you're comfortable speaking out. Your tact track includes learning to assess people and situations before you speak.

If you've chosen a lot of B's, you are cautious and have a gift for watchful waiting. You may prefer to stay away from new situations and you may try to avoid criticism. Your tact track includes improving your direct communication skills and getting more comfortable with speaking directly, when appropriate.

If you've chosen a lot of C's, you are alert to the subtleties of personality. You're good at reading people and good at judging situations. Your tact track includes broadening these skills.

If you've chosen D's, look for opportunities to analyze your communication style and expand your skills accordingly.

Who Are Your Tact Track Teachers?

We've all been in situations where people communicate with more tackiness than tactfulness. We've also been in settings where we feel understood and connected. As part of creating your own Tact Track, look for people who are already experts at communicating with diplomacy and professionalism. See what you can learn from them. Answer these questions about the diplomats in your life. Feel free to list the same person in more than one question.

1. Who makes you feel like you are smart, important and worth listening to? What in their speech, manner or behavior lets you feel this way?

    Name: _____

    Relationship: _____

    Speech, manner or behavior: _____

    Name: _____

    Relationship: _____

    Speech, manner or behavior: _____

    Name: _____

    Relationship: _____

    Speech, manner or behavior: _____

2. Who can you count on, when you're bringing new people together, to help others feel at ease? What in their speech, manner or behavior helps people feel comfortable?

    Name: _____

    Relationship: _____

    Speech, manner or behavior: _____

Name: _____

Relationship: _____

Speech, manner or behavior: _____

Name: _____

Relationship: _____

Speech, manner or behavior: _____

3. When things get touchy, who usually comes up with a problem-solving solution or an idea? What in their speech, manner or behavior allows people to listen to their ideas?

Name: _____

Relationship: _____

Speech, manner or behavior: _____

Name: _____

Relationship: _____

Speech, manner or behavior: _____

Name: _____

Relationship: _____

Speech, manner or behavior: _____

4. Who is comfortable with a variety of people, regardless of age, culture, gender or social class? How do they show their comfort?

Name: _____

Relationship: _____

Speech, manner or behavior: _____

Name: _____

Relationship: _____

Speech, manner or behavior: _____

Name: _____

Relationship: _____

Speech, manner or behavior: _____

5. What are some of the other qualities of your favorite diplomats? (For example, you may enjoy the way one person adds personal stories into a conversation. You may enjoy one person's well-modulated voice or another person's sense of humor.)

1. _____

2. _____

3. _____

4. _____

As you review the above answers, notice any people you listed more than once. These people are masters in the art of diplomacy. One of them may make an excellent mentor for you.

The more you notice the kinds of communications that feel professional and diplomatic to you, the more you can emulate the behaviors and add extra layers of diplomacy into your everyday life.

Your Tact Tracker

As you go through your day, use this simple tact tracker to see how diplomatic you're being:

- **Test** for diplomacy. Before you speak, ask yourself, "Is what I'm going to say true, kind and necessary?"
- **Ask** questions to help you understand more about the person or situation you're dealing with
- **Communicate** slowly, simply and sincerely
- **Thank** people for listening and invite their feedback and ideas
- **Focus** on flexibility and openness as key factors in communicating
- **Understand** the importance of variances in cultural, business and personal communication styles
- **Learn** from each communication and each situation

Here's how Tina used the **TACTFUL** test:

T—Test for Diplomacy

Before you speak, ask yourself, "Is what I'm going to say true, kind and necessary?"

Tina wanted to share some information with Kevin about one of their co-workers, Ruth. Ruth reminded Tina of Carol—she seemed critical and negative. Tina was having a hard time working with this woman and wanted to warn Kevin about her since he was scheduled to have her on his work team. When Tina stopped to test her communication for diplomacy, she came up with these results:

- **Is it true?** The information was true for Tina. It was her personal experience with this colleague.
- **Is it kind?** Tina hesitated on this one. In one sense, Tina was being kind to Kevin, but perhaps she wasn't being kind to Ruth.
- **Is it necessary?** This was another hard one for Tina. She wanted to do Kevin a favor. But really, this was not necessary. Kevin had a lot of communication skills and he'd be able to deal with anyone on his team. Maybe she should let Kevin establish his own relationship with Ruth.

After using the Test for Diplomacy, Tina decided to keep silent on the subject.

A—Ask Questions to Help You Understand More About the Person or Situation You're Dealing With

Since Tina had opted not to discuss Ruth with Kevin, she decided to take action instead. She wanted to know why Ruth seemed to reject new ideas. She hoped that if she asked questions and learned more about Ruth's previous work experience, she'd have a better idea of how to deal with her.

Tina thought about talking to Ruth, but their relationship was prickly. Tina figured Ruth might not trust her enough to share any information. So Tina called a friend of hers who had worked with Ruth at her previous workplace. She asked what the work environment was like. From her friend, Tina learned that their boss was very negative. When anyone tried to introduce new ideas, he or she was criticized. Tina figured that sort of criticism must have made Ruth skittish about introducing or advocating for change. She now understood enough about Ruth to speak to her directly.

C—Communicate Slowly, Simply and Sincerely, Using a Compassionate Tone

Tina wanted to let Ruth know that in this company, new ideas were welcome. Tina knew from earlier feedback that she tended to talk quickly, and she sometimes changed subjects without warning. Tina wrote out an outline of what she wanted to say and practiced beforehand.

She asked Ruth to meet with her and told her she wanted to share some extra information about the company and about this department. Tina communicated slowly and sincerely, sticking with her subject.

T—Thank People for Listening and Invite Feedback and Ideas

Tina noticed that Ruth listened carefully to what she was saying. When she finished speaking, she thanked Ruth for listening and invited feedback, questions and ideas. She wanted to make sure Ruth felt like an important part of the conversation.

"Thanks for clarifying this," Ruth said. "I was concerned that I'd be seen as impractical and unfocused if I embraced some of the ideas people mentioned. But if it's brainstorming and all ideas are welcome, I'll suspend my judgments. I'll also try to contribute some ideas of my own."

F—Focus on Flexibility and Openness as Key Factors in Communicating

Tina felt good after her conversation with Ruth. By asking questions and being open to hearing the answers, she was on the way to resolving her issues with Ruth. By being flexible, she had moved past her initial irritation and into a working relationship with Ruth. She felt hopeful that Ruth would be more open and less negative at their next team meeting.

U—Understand the Importance of Variances in Cultural, Business and Personal Communication Styles

Tina had thought Ruth was being negative and hard to deal with. Ruth, who came from a different business culture, was simply trying to protect herself from negative feedback to get along.

L—Learn From Each Communication and Each Situation

Tina learned that she could not assume everyone had all the information they needed. She had not specifically welcomed new ideas and creative thinking when she introduced the project to Ruth. She would offer more information next time. She also learned the value of asking questions.

Tina was starting to understand how concentrating on diplomatic and professional communication skills could really enhance her working relationships.

As you move through this book, you'll be exploring ways to include such **TACTFUL** tracking to improve your working relationships.

Chapter Two:

Participating in and Leading Productive Meetings

Tina's boss had volunteered her for a task force that was looking at the company's mission and vision statements. As a technical writer, Tina was often a little uncomfortable in these kinds of meetings.

Usually Tina waltzed into a meeting and headed straight toward the coffee. Today, Clara was at the door, greeting everyone. Bright cloth covered the table and each place had an agenda, a pad of paper, sticky notes and a pen.

Clara started the meeting on time. She invited everyone to turn off their cell phones. She introduced herself briefly, saying a few words about her work and adding one thing she liked to do after hours. She invited everyone else to do the same. Tina listened carefully as they went around the table, noting who liked to do gardening, yoga, skydiving, reading and more. Some of the people she knew, others she didn't. She liked knowing something personal about each of them.

"Our goal is to create a draft of ideas that will serve as the core of our updated mission and vision statements," Clara told them.

Clara explained the first brainstorming exercise, briefly outlining the rules of brainstorming. She asked that everyone keep their responses short, offering ideas but not elaborating on them yet. She reminded everyone there were no bad ideas. Then she asked if there were any additional questions.

When the brainstorming began, Tina was surprised to find she had a few ideas. She got carried away and began expounding on one of them.

"Those are great thoughts, Tina," Clara gently interjected. "Can you jot them down and save them for when we do our analysis?"

Tina felt herself blushing—she did tend to get carried away sometimes—but she didn't feel embarrassed. Clara had to remind several other people to stay focused.

Tina noticed how Clara followed the agenda and kept the group moving forward without seeming to rush. Clara also managed to get everyone involved without letting anyone take over.

Tina left the meeting feeling exhilarated. She wanted to incorporate Clara's communications approach into the monthly meeting of technical writers that she co-facilitated.

Clara had used the **MOSAICS** method for facilitating a meeting:

- **Make** people feel welcome and valuable
- **Open** the meeting on time
- **Set** the intention, tone and goal for the meeting
- **Ask** for opinions, comments and questions
- **Include** as many people as possible in the conversation
- **Center** on the agenda; rein in people who talk too long or who wander off topic
- **Stop** on time

MOSAICS Makes the Meeting

The technical writing group met during an extended lunch hour the third Tuesday of each month. About 35 people came. Everyone brought their lunches and ate while Tina and her co-facilitator Steve led the business meeting. Then a guest speaker provided an educational component. Questions and answers followed.

Tina told Steve about the visioning meeting. "I'm up for trying something new," he said. "People get tired of the same old thing, and attendance has been off recently."

Here's how Steve and Tina used **MOSAICS** for their monthly meeting:

M—Make People Feel Welcome and Valuable

Tina stood at the door and greeted people. She smiled when she spoke and used welcoming body language.

"Thanks so much for coming," she said. Or "I'm so glad you're here. I think you're going to enjoy today's topic." She tried to use the **TACTFUL** track, making sure she was speaking diplomatically and sincerely. She wanted to be friendly but not gooey.

Tina enjoyed greeting everyone. In many meetings, she didn't get to talk to each person, and this brief contact made the event seem more personal. Also, because she had connected with each person, she felt her audience would really be with her when she opened the meeting.

Steve stayed inside the meeting room, directing people to open seats and introducing newcomers to some of the long-time members. He wanted to make sure each person had someone to talk to.

O—Open the Meeting On Time

Normally, they let 10 or 15 minutes drag by to allow for stragglers. Today, they started on time. Tina wanted to honor the people who were punctual and encourage the latecomers to arrive sooner next time.

S—Set the Intention, Tone and Goal for the Meeting

The mission meeting Tina had attended had a focused purpose and intention. These monthly meetings were less focused. Still, Steve and Tina reviewed the purpose of these meetings: To bring technical writers together for the purposes of networking, education, problem-solving and keeping abreast in their field. They used the purposes as the basis for their intention and added the educational topic.

"Our goal is to spend this time building our network, increasing our connections and resources and improving technical skills and business skills," Steve told the group. Tina noticed that several people nodded and looked impressed. She herself felt impressed; it was good to be reminded why they were all here.

A—Ask for Opinions, Comments and Questions

Usually people had only a question or two for the speaker. Tina decided to facilitate the question-and-answer sessions, so she could evoke more response.

After the few questions, she asked some additional questions of the audience:

- "How do you see incorporating this information into your workplace?"
- "How many of you have used similar techniques? Let's have a few volunteers tell us how this technique worked for them."

Several people shared ideas and information, and the audience asked them questions.

I—Include as Many People as Possible in the Conversation

Since the group was too large for everyone to participate, Steve designed a quick table exercise to do before leaving. He asked everyone to go around the table, say their name and give one writing or work goal for the next month. Tina liked the buzz of energy the suggestion inspired.

C—Center on the Agenda; Rein in People Who Talk Too Long or Who Wander Off Topic

During the question-and-answer session, one woman rambled on, asking a long, complex question. Tina couldn't think of a diplomatic way to rein her in. Then she remembered what Clara had said to her when she was rambling and gently interrupted the monologue, saying: "That's an excellent point. But I'm afraid we're running out of time, so perhaps we could continue the conversation after the meeting."

Tina hoped she didn't sound rude. She decided that next time, she'd ask people to keep their remarks brief; that way, she would feel more comfortable interrupting if she needed to.

S—Stop On Time

Tina ended the question-and-answer session five minutes early, so they'd have time for the table exercise. Steve ended the meeting on time.

Several people stopped by to praise the meeting. "I liked the last exercise," one woman said. "In fact, I wouldn't mind having a meeting that's all networking."

Afterwards, Steve and Tina talked over the meeting. They agreed that asking for ideas and opinions had shown that the members would enjoy more chances to have professional dialogue with each other.

"Maybe we could have panel discussions at some meetings instead of a speaker," Steve suggested. "We could also have a quick exercise at the beginning of the meeting instead of at the end."

They also brainstormed ways to curtail nonstop or off-topic talkers. Steve had a lot of experience on this subject. He suggested:

- Telling people in advance: "We want to involve as many of you as possible, so please keep your remarks brief."
- Interrupting if a person gets off the subject, with, "We're running short on time. How does this relate to … (the topic at hand)?"
- Interrupting when a person is taking over by saying, "Thanks for all your ideas, but I'm going to ask you to stop for now so we can have some comments from others."

  Or …

  "You've made a lot of valuable comments. Can you wrap up your remarks in one minute?"

Both Tina and Steve agreed, the **MOSAICS** meeting map had added extra structure, participation and connection to what had become a routine gathering.

Tact Tip:

As the facilitator, ask people to raise their hand before speaking. This assures everyone an equal chance of contributing.

Professional Pointer:

If people are slow showing up at meetings, dedicate the first 10 minutes to networking or education. Make those ten minutes valuable for those who are on time so, instead of just waiting, they're getting connected and informed.

The Woolly Mammoth Meeting

Some meeting styles should be as extinct as the woolly mammoth. Courtney was trapped in one, and she was making a list of the things that drove her crazy about this meeting. The list read:

- No agenda
- Starts late
- People interrupt
- People talk on and on
- People get off the topic
- People never look up and never give eye contact
- People tell inside stories or use obscure acronyms
- Some people just sit there and never say a word

She had to admit, she herself was one of those just-sit-there people. But that had to be better than being one of those talk-all-the-time people. Still, when she had talked to Tina last week about how to be more professional, Tina had mentioned participating in meetings.

"It's a chance to be noticed," Tina had told her.

But Courtney figured she was too bored and irritated to say anything useful in this meeting. And she figured she really didn't count.

"You do count," Tina later told her. "Every person in the meeting can make a difference if she wants to. The participants have as much to contribute as the facilitators do."

Courtney was skeptical, but Tina persuaded her to give it a try. Tina gave Courtney a short list of ways she could participate. "I made this **PASS** list from watching people in meetings," Tina said. "You can learn a lot about professional communication that way. You can also learn a lot about unprofessional communication!"

Tina's list included:

- **Prepare.** If the facilitator doesn't send out an agenda, ask for one. That way, you can be prepared to comment in at least one area. If you can, find out how many people are coming and who they are. This will help you understand your audience.

- **Assert yourself.** Sometimes you have to speak up or gesture to get attention in a meeting. If you're shy, ask a colleague to help you get a word in edgewise. Listen carefully and make sure you understand the intention of the meeting. Ideally, your remarks will contribute to the goal.

- **Speak clearly, confidently and briefly.** Ask clarifying questions when needed. The more information you have, the more you can contribute.

- **Speak diplomatically.** Use the Test for Diplomacy. Don't use terminology or acronyms that your audience doesn't understand. Try to refer back to something somebody else said that honors the speaker, shows off your listening skills and encourages others to be inclusive.

Leading From the Middle

Every week, Courtney attended a departmental meeting. She usually felt these meetings were a waste of time. Nobody ever asked her opinion and she never offered any information. But Tina had said, "You know a lot about how things are run. You could definitely make a mark in those meetings."

So Courtney decided to try. One of the agenda items was about controlling e-mails. Courtney had training on this subject and felt confident talking about it.

At the meeting, she listened attentively, eagerly awaiting the e-mail topic. As she listened, she also heard other areas where she felt she had something to say. But she waited.

Several people poured out their opinions about "e-mail overwhelm," mainly complaining. Each time Courtney started to speak, someone edged her out. She remembered what Tina said about asserting herself. The facilitator was winding down the conversation, but Courtney raised her hand and said, "I have a comment."

Keeping her tone confident, she mentioned a few of the e-mail-reducing techniques she had learned. Then she said, "As you may know, I serve as an assistant for several departments. If you like, I can find out what other departments are doing to reduce time spent on e-mail and report back at the next meeting."

"Thank you, Courtney. We'll look forward to that report," the facilitator said. Courtney felt a flush of happiness. This was the first time someone had acknowledged her in this meeting. Of course, this was also the first time she had spoken up.

Professional Pointer:

If you don't feel comfortable speaking spontaneously, volunteer to provide information or a report that you can prepare. This gives you a chance to participate with confidence.

What Makes Meetings Marvelous?

Usually, Courtney walked out of the department meeting feeling drained and incompetent. Now she felt energized and empowered. She had a task and she would do it well, which would contribute to her company's efficiency.

Courtney called Tina and said, "It worked. I spoke in the meeting and now I've volunteered to do something, so I'll have to speak in the next meeting."

What makes you walk out of a meeting feeling as if you've accomplished something? As you sit through various gatherings, make mental notes about the styles of communication that work best for you. Then create your own "Best Meeting" list, writing down the components that make a meeting work for you. Use this list to help you be a better participant and a better facilitator.

Here's part of Courtney's list:

1. An agenda, so I have a chance to prepare

2. Someone to greet me and welcome me, so I feel important

3. A chance to speak

4. A chance to take action, so I feel like I'm contributing

5. Someone actually calling on me to speak, so I don't have to butt in

6. A facilitator who keeps everyone on track, so when someone starts a long rant, she stops it

Steve's list included:

1. A round of introductions, so I know the name and title of everyone at the meeting

2. A timeline for each agenda item

3. A facilitator who asks for final comments on each item

4. In ongoing large meetings, small-group sessions so people get to know each other better

Think of great meetings you've attended and add other components that contribute to a well-run and effective meeting:

1._____

2._____

3._____

4._____

5._____

Measuring Your Meetings

Whether you are a facilitator or participant, it's worth analyzing meetings and your performance to see how you can improve your own professional and diplomatic communication skills. The more visible you are, the more people will come to value your presence and your ideas.

For each meeting, set a goal for yourself. The goal may be simply to say one thing. Or to keep to the agenda. Or to share an important idea you want to get support for. Or to speak to several of your co-workers. You can always ask for the support of another participant in reaching your goal. If you find it hard to speak out, ask a compassionate co-worker to sit next to you and help you be heard. If you find it hard to speak succinctly, ask a co-worker to make a subtle gesture if you start going on too long.

Here are some other questions to ask yourself:

- **How can I make the meeting more successful?**
  For example, you can suggest brief introductions with everyone mentioning one thing they like to do outside of work or one magazine they like to read.

- **What can I offer to do to become more a part of the meeting?**
  You can volunteer to greet people as they enter. You can volunteer to bring a snack. You can volunteer to synopsize an article that would benefit the participants.

- **How can I come across more professionally?**
  You can speak when you have something to say. You can listen attentively when others are speaking.

- **How can I contribute to a more efficient and effective meeting?**
  You can be on time. You can make sure you stay on topic.

- **How can I inspire others to get more interested and involved?**
  You can ask questions of people who haven't spoken, but who have knowledge in the area.

Remember, the more you bring **MOSAICS** into each meeting, the more dynamic the meeting.

- <u>**Make**</u> people feel welcomed and valuable
- <u>**Open**</u> the meeting on time
- <u>**Set**</u> the intention, tone and goal for the meeting
- <u>**Ask**</u> for opinions, comments and questions
- <u>**Include**</u> as many people as possible in the conversation
- <u>**Center**</u> on the agenda, reining in people who talked too long or who wander off topic
- <u>**Stop**</u> on time

Chapter Three:

Giving Great Presentations

"Try it again," Steve said.

"We've been working on this for two hours!" Tina complained. "Yesterday, I worked for four hours. I can't believe I'm spending so much time on a 15-minute presentation."

Steve had asked Tina to give a short presentation on "Adding Spice to Instructional Manuals" at their monthly technical writers group meeting. She was known for her ability to create readable manuals.

When Tina said, "I don't usually speak to groups that large," Steve volunteered to coach her. Steve had attended Toastmasters for years and had a lot of experience with both speaking and facilitating.

Now, Tina was wishing she had never agreed to this presentation. The thought of speaking in front of 35 people was making her nervous. And Steve's insistence that she diligently prepare and practice her speech made her even more nervous.

"I know this stuff off the top of my head," she told him.

"Yes, but can you communicate the information in a way that others will easily understand and remember? For example, tell me in two sentences what your speech is about."

"Well, it's about making sure that you, as a technical writer, have the tools or maybe understand the tools you need to be able to add in, you know, some well, some ... "

"You've already lost me," Steve told her.

The GIFT of Presentations

"You are here to give the audience a gift—information that will benefit them," Steve told her. "You are also here to receive a gift—35 people paying attention to you, noticing who you are and what you know. What an opportunity."

Tina thought about that. This was a great networking opportunity, a chance to share her skills and knowledge and to be visible among a group of her peers. She knew it was a great opportunity, and she decided to make the most of it, despite her fears and concerns.

Steve outlined the **GIFT** of presentations:

- **Get** the audience's attention
- **Illustrate** your points with personal stories
- **Feature** three key points (or fewer) in your presentation
- **Tell** the audience the benefits and give them a take-away

Steve worked with Tina on each one of the components:

G—Get the Audience's Attention

At most meetings Tina attended, the speaker started out by saying something like "Thanks for having me," "This is a great group. It's great to be here" or something equally bland.

Steve told her: "At the opening of your presentation, every split second counts. This is your chance to get the audience's attention. This is your chance to get them interested in you and your speech. Plan an opening that makes the audience want to know more."

Tina thought of a note of praise she had received from a contented client. She had laughed when she read it and thought her audience of tech writers might also get a kick out of it. She thought of saying:

"Two years ago I received an e-mail from a client that changed my life and enriched my bank account." Then Tina would read from a piece of paper: "'Dear Tina, this is the best instructional manual I have ever read. I only had to drink two cups of coffee to get through it—and they were DECAF!'"

"During the 15 next minutes, I'm going to share the three reasons I received this e-mail. These are techniques for putting more spice into your technical writing. With these simple techniques, you'll have more fun writing, you'll create more usable manuals and you'll create greater client satisfaction. And if you're lucky, as I was, you'll also experience monetary gain!"

Professional Pointer:

A great opening includes something that grabs the listeners' attention, information on how the listener will benefit from this presentation, a promise of the content to come and a splash of humor and personality.

I—Illustrate Your Points With Personal Stories

Tina wanted to plunge right into her techniques, but Steve suggested she further engage her audience by adding a short personal story.

"Adding in a personal story is an easy way to make yourself a memorable speaker," Steve told her. He told her that many businesses encouraged the use of personal storytelling in meetings and presentations. "Through stories," he said, "you can motivate, engage and inspire while delivering valuable information."

Tina liked the idea but had no clue where to begin.

"I can't think of any story that has any relevance to technical writing," she said.

"Let's think about conflicts," Steve suggested. "For example, did you have any resistance when you first started incorporating these techniques? Did it take extra time and energy?"

"Oh gosh, that project seemed to eat up my time. But I was determined to struggle on through and write a manual that was interesting," Tina replied. "I was constantly asking myself, 'Is it worth it?' Plus, I had a new puppy and I was having a hard time training him. I was also asking myself if the puppy was worth all the extra work."

Steve encouraged Tina to create a story that included the puppy and the new writing skills, centered on the theme: "Is it worth it?"

He worked with Tina so her story included four parts:

1. **The hero wants something.** Tina was the hero. She wanted a trained puppy, and she wanted better writing skills.

2. **Something or someone is in the hero's way.** For Tina, time and uncertainty were in her way. She also had a deadline-oriented boss who did not appreciate the extra time she was taking to make the manual more readable. She also doubted her own creative abilities.

3. **The hero perseveres, overcomes obstacles and solves the problem.** Tina solved her problems by not giving up, by letting herself be imperfect and by trying various techniques, both with her dog and with her writing.

4. **The hero celebrates with a happy ending.** Tina had an adorable, well-behaved puppy, and she received a great note, plus a bonus from her boss.

As Tina practiced her story, Steve gave her some tips to get **AHEAD** with her storytelling:

- **Add in audience involvement.** Ask questions that encourage people to raise their hand, such as, "How many of you have ever experienced that wrenching feeling of doubt?"

- **Have a laugh at yourself and increase the humor.** Use specific detail. Tell the audience how you propped yourself up with chocolate and lattes, fighting against the writing deadline and against your uncertainty about whether you could write a more readable manual.

- **Engage the senses.** As much as you can, include visual descriptions as well as sounds, tastes, smells and textures.

- **Acknowledge and show your emotions.** Try to select situations and emotions your audience can identify with.

- **Deal in dialogue.** Dialogue spices up the story and lets you use voices and gestures in a playful way.

With Steve's help, Tina added her personal story into the opening of her speech:

"Two years ago I received an e-mail from a client that changed my life and enriched my bank account."

Then Tina would read from a piece of paper: "'Dear Tina, this is the best instructional manual I have ever read. I only had to drink two cups of coffee to get through it—and they were DECAF!'

"During the 15 next minutes, I'm going to talk about the three simple techniques that inspired this e-mail. When you incorporate these easy techniques, you can put more spice into your technical writing, have more fun writing and create greater client satisfaction. And if you're as lucky as I was, you'll also experience monetary gain!

"But first, I want to take you back to when I was first experimenting with these new techniques. I was on a deadline and already worn out because I had a new puppy at home. A naughty, shoe-chewing puppy that needed training, and, unfortunately, couldn't read a manual to get it."

Tina worked hard on creating a three- to five-minute story. Then she practiced the story in front of friends and family, fine-tuning it and getting comfortable with the telling of it.

Creating Your Own Story

Think of presentations you remember and admire. Think about the kinds of stories the presenters told. A good story has a universal theme, shows the readers something about themselves, is short and visual and engages the senses. In a good personal story, the speaker shares something about herself.

Think of a presentation you have coming up. This could be as simple as reporting at a meeting or making a speech. As you think about creating a story, ask yourself:

1. What is the theme of my presentation?

2. Who is my audience? Describe the types of people in your audience, including age range, gender, job titles and more.

3. What kinds of life experiences will the audience most identify with? Think about areas that people identify with such as pets, food, sports and deadlines. List several:

   - _____

   - _____

   - _____

   - _____

4. What words, phrases or slogans can I use to tie my life experience to the theme of my presentation? For example, Tina used, "Is it worth it?" as her tie-in.

   Steve had chosen the slogan "What if I fail?" to illustrate his experience running a marathon. He tied that theme into his work issue of trying to launch a new product. Within the speech, he moved from "What if I fail?" to "What if I succeed?" Try any ideas that come to you—don't worry about perfection when you're starting.

5. Who can I practice on? List people you feel comfortable with. Practice your story on them. Ask for feedback. As you tell the story, notice when they light up and when they drift away.

My practice team:

1. _____

2. _____

3. _____

4. _____

F—Feature Three Key Points (or Fewer) in Your Presentation

"I have too much to say," Tina told Steve as she worked on the body of her presentation. "I have a million little tips that don't really fit under just three categories."

"Think about the speaker last month," Steve said. "What do you remember about her presentation?"

Tina stopped and thought. Sometime during the presentation, the speaker told a little story about a cat that Tina somehow remembered. The story was fun, but Tina had thought it was too long. She also remembered one of the resources the speaker recommended. That was all.

"OK," she said. "You're right. I'll figure out the three points."

It's All About *You* Being All About *Them*

When you're preparing for your speech, think about the audience first. As people listen to your speech, they're thinking, "What's in this for me? How does this information benefit me?"

Of course you're eager to share your wisdom and knowledge. To create an effective speech, consider the information you most want to share and how it will benefit the audience. Then consider how much information the audience can take in.

With Steve's help, Tina grouped her ideas under three main techniques. She found key words that started with R, so she could title the segment *The Three R's of Readability*. She treated each R like it was a mini-speech and included:

- Dynamic openings
- Short, simple sentences, free of jargon and clichés
- Storytelling techniques, trying to keep her talk visual and engaging
- Benefits to the audience

T—Tell the Audience the Benefits and Give Them a Take-away

Tina set up her benefits in the introduction when she said: "With these simple techniques, you'll have more fun writing and create greater client satisfaction. And if you're as lucky as I was, you'll also experience monetary gain!"

She listed those benefits again at the end of the speech and added others, which included: Becoming more memorable; gaining more confidence as you explore your creative nature; helping your clients become more efficient, since there's more chance of people reading the manuals if they're fun to read; and being asked to give presentations like this one.

Then she added an extra take-away—a sound bite.

Give Them Something to Chew On—a Sound Bite

Imagine someone leaving your presentation, calling a friend and saying, "I just heard the most fascinating presentation. It was about … " Then imagine the sentence or two they will say.

Along with the personal story, the sound bite helps people remember you and your presentation.

Tina soon discovered that sound bites take a while to create. She tried several variations:

- *This has been a speech about adding creativity to a technical product*
- *Adding your creative touch to a technical writing project can make you memorable*
- *People will remember you and your instructional manual when you take the time and talent to add in your creative touch*
- *Readability rocks! Even when you are writing something unspeakably dull, you can add in a little humor and spice to keep the reading nice*
- *Go from mousy to magnificent when you add the Three Rs of Readability to your technical writings*

She tested her bites on various people, asking them to pick the two they liked the best. Courtney chose "Readability Rocks."

"It sounds trendy and cool," she said.

Ruth, who was more conservative, preferred "Adding your creative touch to a technical writing project can make you memorable."

Kevin liked "the Three R's of Readability," but thought "Mousy to Magnificent" was a bit too exaggerated.

They all rejected "This has been a speech about adding creativity to a technical product" as too boring. Tina later realized there was no hook or benefit for the audience in that bite. Tina decided to combine their comments and created her sound bite:

> *"People will remember you and your instructional manuals when you add the Three Rs of Readability to your technical writings. Remember—Readability Rocks!"*

The sound bite was short, included an audience benefit and referred to the content of Tina's speech, her three techniques.

She continued to try it out on people to see if she could fine-tune it even further.

She also gave her audience another take-away—an action challenge. She invited them to add at least one of the three readability components to their next project.

"If you get stuck or discouraged, you can e-mail me a page, and I'll be happy to give you some direction or feedback," Tina planned to say. This was the kind of help Tina wished had been available to her.

Stage Coaching: Giving the Speech

Tina had never been so prepared in her life. She knew her subject matter, and she'd practiced her speech many times on family and friends and with Steve. The room was filling with her colleagues, other technical writers, most of whom she knew. So why were her palms sweating and her heart racing? Why did she want to throw her notes at Steve and run out of the room?

"It's normal to feel nervous," Steve said, when he noticed how pale she was. "Take some deep breaths. See yourself receiving a huge round of applause when the speech is over."

Tina breathed. She smiled at the thought of that round of applause. When she took the microphone, her voice was shaking. Then she remembered what Steve had taught her about eye contact: Keep connected with the audience by looking at people while you speak. She looked at a friend who was smiling encouragingly at her. Then she looked at another friend. Before she knew it, she was hearing that applause she had envisioned.

"Great information," one person said afterwards.

"I loved the puppy story," another said. "I have a dog myself."

"I'm going to share the readability tips with my department," another said. "We might want you to come speak to us."

Tina left the meeting feeling she had both given and received a **GIFT**. Her gift was seeing how much people enjoyed the information, how complimentary they were and how intently they listened to her speech.

Over the weeks that followed, Tina saw more benefits from her presentation. Two department heads from other companies asked her to speak to their technical writing teams and offered to pay her a modest honorarium. When Ruth learned about Tina's talk, she said, "In my old company, whenever anyone spoke for an outside group, they put a blurb in the company newsletter." Tina wrote up a blurb and asked Ruth for editing comments. Ruth had a few suggestions and advised, "Send a picture with it." The newsletter published both blurb and picture, so Tina received a lot of visibility and a lot of nice feedback within her own company.

Professional Pointer:

Before a speech, put yourself at ease. Take a few moments to get centered. Breathe deeply if you are feeling nervous. Some speakers create an affirmation they use, such as "I speak easily and gracefully. I connect fully with the audience."

Tact Tip:

When you're speaking, try to greet and talk to your audience members before your speech. This will make you feel more like you're talking to friends. If you're quite nervous, ask a few people to give you encouraging smiles as you speak. Then look at them when you feel uncomfortable.

Becoming an "Expert"—More Benefits of Presenting

The presentation had also benefited Tina by:

- Helping her hone her ideas and tips into three easy techniques
- Making her into more of an "expert" on her subject
- Increasing her public speaking skills and her professional confidence
- Giving her visibility in the workplace and within her profession
- Inspiring her to look at her work and notice other techniques she was using

GIFT Certificate—Presentation Checklist:

As you put together your presentation, ask yourself: "Do I have … ":

- *Someone in mind?* The audience
- *Somewhere in mind?* The room you're presenting in
- *Some way to get their attention?* The opening WOW
- *Some way they'll remember me?* The personal story
- *Something for them to learn?* Three points
- *Something for them to do?* The take-away or call to action
- *Something for them to tell others?* The sound bite
- *Something that involves?* The benefits

Whether you're speaking at a small meeting or for a large group, presenting is a **GIFT**, an opportunity to make yourself memorable and remarkable.

- **Get** the audience's attention
- **Illustrate** your points with personal stories
- **Feature** three key points (or less) in your presentation
- **Tell** the audience the benefits and give them a take-away

Chapter Four:

Influencing and Persuading Others

"Oh no," Courtney murmured as she glanced through her e-mails before heading out to lunch. "Another eco-blast from Kevin."

This one was about the environmental impact of eating beef. Courtney looked guiltily at the roast beef sandwich she had brought for lunch and decided tomorrow she'd bring egg salad. Last week, he sent something about plastic bottles and landfills, and she wondered if she should hide her bottle of spring water. She appreciated some of the information Kevin shared, but she thought this barrage of eco-e-mails was a bit overwhelming.

In the lunch room, Kevin waved her over. Just her luck, she would have to eat her beef sandwich right in front of the vegan. And she was carrying a plastic bottle of water, which she knew would soon be cluttering up a landfill.

"I want your advice," Kevin said. "I'm trying to promote more environmental awareness around here, maybe start a recycling program and give people more information on how they can make a difference. But so far, nobody seems too interested. Any advice?"

Courtney looked at Kevin and thought about what she wanted to say. Kevin usually was quite skilled at communicating. But on this subject, he came across as overzealous.

"Maybe you could be less bombarding and more persuasive," Courtney told him. "I'm interested in the information, but when I read your e-mails, I feel like I'm being scolded."

Kevin nodded thoughtfully as he ate his avocado-and-tomato sandwich. His wife had said the same thing just last week. So had another colleague. Maybe he needed to learn more about the fine art of influencing and persuading.

The I's Have It: Influencing Others

Kevin realized he had not been thinking of others when he sent his environmental e-mails. He was burning with a desire to create change, and he figured everyone would be glad to receive the information. But Courtney's comments made him realize he needed to change his approach.

Normally, Kevin was a diplomatic communicator. He liked to listen to people, to understand their personalities and their needs, before he spoke. He tried to use the **TACTFUL** approach (See Chapter 1). But regarding the environment, somehow he had gotten off the Tact Track.

Now he thought about the steps he often took when he wanted to influence his team or get his point across at a meeting. His usual approach was **The I's Have It**. He wrote down the seven I's he used as a guide to influencing others:

1. **Identify** the results you want
2. **Illustrate** your credibility
3. **Invest** time in getting to know the person or people you want to persuade
4. **Invite** their ideas and involve them in your quest
5. **Investigate** options where you might meet on common ground
6. **Intend** an outcome that meets everyone's needs
7. **Improvise** as needed

Then, he deleted the e-mail he had planned to send about the benefits of using recycled paper and began creating a strategic plan based on the I's.

Identify the Results You Want

Kevin had several goals. He wanted to feel that he was making a difference in the workplace. He wanted to reduce waste at work. He wanted to create a community of people who were interested in the environment and who would work with him to make their workplace greener. He wanted to get more involved in Community Affairs, with a long-term goal of working in that area. As a side benefit, he knew that being more active environmentally would help set his company apart in the community.

To identify measurable results, he wrote:

- I want to create a team that will work with me on company-wide recycling
- I want to set up recycling areas for paper, plastic and cans
- I want to see if there's interest in monthly brown bag seminars to discuss how individuals can make a difference
- I want to see if there's interest in receiving a monthly e-letter with easy individual environmental tips

Illustrate Your Credibility

"What gives you the right to tell me how to eat?" a co-worker had asked him when Kevin mentioned the environmental impact of beef.

Now Kevin realized the guy had a point. Only six months earlier, Kevin had enjoyed hamburgers and ribs at the company picnic. He had been recycling for only two years and studying environmental impact for just a year. He had only been a vegetarian for five months. Why would anyone listen to him?

Normally, Kevin would not have tried to influence someone in a field where he was not an expert. But Kevin wanted to create change *now*. Perhaps it was enough that he was just another super-busy person trying to make a difference.

Professional Pointer:

There are many ways to build your "expert" status:

- Share information by publishing tips or articles in local newsletters or periodicals
- Volunteer to present at meetings or to give speeches on the subject
- Align with another expert
- Get testimonials from people who have used your ideas or services

Invest Time in Getting to Know Those You Want to Persuade

Kevin knew the people he had e-mailed, some better than others. But he knew most of them primarily through work and didn't know much about their ideas about the greening of the workplace.

He put together a couple of questions to ask people—open-ended, non-judgmental questions that would help him learn more about his audience:

- Do you have any concerns regarding the environment?
- What are some of them?
- What are some of the ways you'd like to make a difference?

Since his e-mails had possibly irritated some people, he decided to use the old-fashioned approach and actually talk to people face to face. He did this at lunch, on break and before meetings. He opened the conversations casually, talking about his own quest to do something, even though he was practically too busy to breathe.

"I'm trying to figure out a few things I can do without giving up any work, personal or family time. What about you—what are some of your concerns? What kinds of things are you doing along those lines?"

He was surprised and impressed with the results.

Courtney donated her old shoes and clothes to a women's employment program. Tina recycled everything at home. Ruth recycled her books to the library. One person bought only recycled paper and inks. Another avoided plastic bags. Kevin listened carefully and made notes of these tips.

Within three weeks, he'd gathered information from about 20 people. He realized most people were willing to do something as long as it didn't cost too much in time, money or personal pleasure. He also realized he was the same way.

Invite Their Ideas and Involve Them in Your Quest

He asked each person for permission to include their tips in a small group e-mail. Then Kevin created an e-mail that went only to the people he had talked to. The e-mail included the tips, including proper credit to each person. He thanked everyone for their help and asked who would like to be part of a team that worked with management on setting up recycling opportunities at work. Five people were interested. Other people, who couldn't participate, asked to be kept on the e-mail list, and a few volunteered to help later.

At the initial brainstorming meeting, Kevin asked the question: "What would be the easiest, most effective ways to get recycling started?"

One person mentioned a local nonprofit group that worked with businesses on setting up their program. Someone else mentioned simple bins for recycling paper and suggested having lots of them, so people didn't have to walk too far. The same with plastic and cans.

Another person worried that recycling would take up too much time. Another didn't want an ugly blue bin in her office. They talked about how the bins would get emptied and realized they had more work to do before submitting their ideas to management. One person volunteered to interview several middle managers to see if they were interested in being part of the brainstorming team. Another suggested interviewing the maintenance staff.

Kevin kept the conversation flowing by continuing to ask questions and invite ideas.

Investigate Options Where You Might Meet on Common Ground

At their next meeting, an expert from the nonprofit group came. The expert showed them statistics on how this kind of program could have no or low cost and how it also improved employee morale and increased visibility in the community. He also gave them tips for keeping the program streamlined, so it wouldn't be too much extra time for any person or department.

"Being seen as a responsible part of the community is important for many businesses," the expert told them. He described several businesses that had been recycling for years and gave them contact information.

Intend an Outcome That Meets Everyone's Needs

Kevin and his team now had information from the nonprofit expert and the other businesses that had started a recycling program. He felt they understood the issues and concerns management might have about starting such a program. They were ready to talk to management and discuss an outcome that met everyone's needs.

Kevin volunteered to start with his boss, Helen. He had once seen an *Audubon* magazine on her desk. He thought a one-on-one meeting with her might be the most effective way to introduce the idea.

Kevin used the **GIFT** approach for his recycling presentation to management, making sure he had an attention-getting opening, a compelling personal story, three key points and benefits for his audience.

Professional Pointer:

As Kevin worked to influence people, he was also honing his speaking, facilitating, leadership, collaborative and networking skills.

Tact Tip:

The more meetings Kevin ran, the more he understood the benefits of listening and involving others. As he heard others share ideas, he could often shape his own thoughts so they were collaborative rather than competitive.

Improvise as Needed

Helen listened carefully to Kevin's presentation.

"I like the idea and I'm happy to help out by having a bin in my office, but I'm too busy to do anything more right now," Helen told him. "If you're willing to explain the program and do some educational sessions, I'll see if some of the other managers are interested in getting involved."

Kevin had hoped for full-out management support.

"What if I write a draft letter for you to include in the newsletter next month?" he asked. "I'll put in the statistics and the experiences of other companies. You can simply edit and sign it. Once people know you're behind this, they'll be more willing to learn more."

Helen agreed.

Putting Influence to Work for You

Practicing your influencing and persuading skills prepares you for many situations, including negotiating, saying no and communicating under pressure. As you think about your own areas of influence, analyze your current persuasion practice. Using **The I's Have It** as a guide, ask yourself:

- In what areas am I an effective influencer?

  1. _____

  2. _____

  3. _____

- In what areas do I need to improve?

  1. _____

  2. _____

  3. _____

Focus on improving in those areas as you create your own "The I's Have It" plan

1. Think of an area in which you'd like to further your influence. Describe the situation. This can be anything from changing the time of a meeting to creating a committee.

   _____

   _____

   _____

   _____

2. Write down the steps you'll need to take, using **The I's Have It** as a model:

   - Identify the results you want

   _____

   - Illustrate your credibility

   _____

   - Invest time in getting to know the person or people you want to persuade

   _____

   - Invite their ideas and involve them in your quest

   _____

   - Investigate options where you might meet on common ground

   _____

   - Intend an outcome that meets everyone's needs

   _____

   - Improvise as needed

   _____

3. List the benefits you'll gain in widening your influence. Some of those benefits might include "improves communications abilities" and "increases networking opportunities."

_____

_____

_____

The Final I—Impress for Success

Learning to influence people went far beyond throwing facts and figures at them. Kevin had learned that influencing was as much about listening and involving as it was about speaking and persuading.

The I's Have It—an I-deal Way of Influencing:

1. **Identify** the results you want

2. **Illustrate** your credibility

3. **Invest** time in getting to know the person or people you want to persuade

4. **Invite** their ideas and involve them in your quest

5. **Investigate** options where you might meet on common ground

6. **Intend** an outcome that meets everyone's needs

7. **Improvise** as needed

Chapter Five:

Communicating Under Pressure

That morning, everyone received a memo stating that their company was negotiating a merger with an East Coast company. "There will be inevitable changes in employee status and in job parameters," the interoffice e-mail said. Helen, one of their VPs, had scheduled an interdepartmental meeting that afternoon so she could talk to everyone about the proposed changes.

Tina felt the tension and worry as she walked into the auditorium. That same anxiety had permeated her department all day.

When Helen strode to the stage, there was a moment of pure silence. Then Tina heard a buzz of voices. Many people raised their hands.

"I know you're all concerned, and I'm sorry you have to deal with this kind of uncertainty," Helen said.

Tina was amazed at Helen's poise.

"I also have to tell you straight out that I don't have all the answers yet," Helen continued. "The merger team is still negotiating the terms of the agreement. Any questions I can't answer now, I'll forward to the executive team. They promised they'll have an update for us by the end of next week."

The noise level dimmed. Some hands went down.

"Let me tell you what I know. Then I'll take questions. First, you'll all be happy to hear that the proposed merger will not impact our current health care coverage. Also … "

Tina listened as Helen described what she knew about situation and then invited questions.

When Helen did not have an answer, she did not seem upset or embarrassed by her lack of knowledge. She simply said, "That's an excellent question. I'll make sure I take that to the team." Or, "Thanks for asking that." Or, "I wondered that myself. That is a concern I think we'll have to put aside until we see the actual terms of the agreement."

Some questions were hostile.

But Helen answered every one of them calmly, saying, "I hear your concern. I hope I can get you an answer soon." Or, "Tell me more about what kind of information you're seeking. I want to make sure I understand your question."

By the end of the meeting, Tina noticed that people seemed calmer. Helen's own calm and understanding tone had made a difference.

Helen ended the meeting by giving people an e-mail address to post further questions. She promised to schedule another meeting next week. She also thanked everyone for their good questions and their patience.

The Recipe for the Pressure Cooker

Ever since Helen had learned about the merger the previous afternoon, she had been trying to understand as much as possible. She knew everyone would be upset. The HR director told her, "I don't envy you, having to talk to people with so little information."

Still, Helen knew rumors could destroy workplace efficiency. She had to open the channels of communication—with or without the necessary information. Helen would rely on her own recipe for communicating under pressure. She called it **HEATING**:

- **H**onesty
- **E**mpathy
- **A**cknowledgment
- **T**ime frame
- **I**nformation
- **N**ext steps
- **G**ratitude

Professional Pointer:

Attitude is everything. The more confidently and honestly you communicate, the less it matters what you know.

HEATING Up the Workplace

After the meeting, Courtney went into Tina's office.

"Are we still employed?" she asked.

"Yes. And remember, sometimes these mergers don't even go through."

"Do you think they'll keep us all on?" Courtney asked. She paced Tina's small office, her hands knotted up, her face frowning.

Tina realized that the people who reported to her might come to her with questions. She knew nothing more than they did, but she knew she needed to be there for them.

She reviewed the way Helen had talked to everyone, analyzing each component of the **HEATING** approach:

H—Honesty

Speak openly and honestly as soon as possible. Even if you don't have all the answers, let people know you intend to get them.

Helen had arranged to speak honestly and instantly. For Tina, just knowing she was going to hear the information from Helen, someone she trusted, helped her manage her feelings of uncertainty. Helen was also honest in saying she didn't have all the answers.

E—Empathy

Establish an atmosphere of connection, concern and caring.

Helen instantly established an atmosphere of connection, concern and caring. She let them know she would listen to their questions.

A—Acknowledgment

Let people know their questions are important. Answer or follow up on all questions.

Helen listened calmly to everyone and made sure her assistant wrote down each question she could not answer. She asked for clarification when she didn't understand a question. She responded to each question in some way, even when she didn't have an answer.

T—Time frame

Tell people when they can expect more information.

Helen told them they would have answers by next week. That made Tina feel there would be an end to the uncertainty.

I—Information

Tell people which experts will supply the information.

Helen told them who would be providing the information. She also made it clear she was available and would facilitate getting all questions answered.

N—Next steps

Let people know the next step, even if it's just another meeting.

Helen set up another meeting. She also offered a way to post other questions and concerns.

G—Gratitude

Thank people in advance for being patient.

Helen thanked people for their insight and patience.

As the day progressed, Tina used some of the **HEATING** components in communicating with her own team.

Tact Tip:

When the stress builds, take a brief centering break. Take three deep breaths. Listen to a song you like. Take a short walk, even if it's just up and down the hallway. Call a friend for support. This one- to two-minute "Time Out" can help you maintain your poise and professionalism.

Thinking (and Talking) on Your Feet

Be prepared. Do your homework. Always have an answer.

Those phrases were marching through Tina's head as she sat in her normal departmental meeting, staring at Charles. He had asked her a question about last year's project and her mind was blank. She couldn't think of a thing to say. So she blurted out, "I don't know."

"I wanted to fall into a hole after I said that," she told Steve later that afternoon. "I must have sounded like an idiot. I got put on the spot, and I couldn't think."

"Actually, it's kind of refreshing to have someone admit they don't know something," Steve said. "But I do have some ideas for you."

Steve offered these tips:

1. When you don't know an answer, buy yourself more time to think of one. To do this:

   - Repeat the question
   - Ask for further clarification
   - Praise the question
   - Say, "That's an interesting question. I need a moment to think about it."

2. To diplomatically acknowledge what you don't know, say:

   - "I'm not familiar with that theory, but it sounds interesting."
   - "That's not information I have off the top of my head, but I'm happy to find the answer and get back with you."
   - "You've brought up a great question; I'll be happy to find that answer."

3. To transfer responsibility for the topic to someone else:

   - "I don't have that information. Perhaps someone else has the answer to that question."
   - "That's a fascinating concept. It's not in my area of expertise, but I imagine HR has the information you seek."
   - "That's the kind of information that could help a lot of people. What about sending out an e-mail to see who has answers?"

4. To change the subject:

- "That sounds like something we need to take up at another meeting."
- "Thanks for bringing that up. Marketing is handling those issues. Let's stay focused on … "

It's Not My Fault—or Is It?

Ruth had just spent 30 minutes arguing with herself about how to approach Greg. Just yesterday, Greg had walked into Ruth's office and accused Ruth of being behind deadline on an important project.

"That project is right on time," Ruth told him, standing up and putting her hands on her hips. "If anyone is causing a delay, it's someone from your team."

"My team is on schedule. Take a look at your timeline, Ruth. Believe me, if someone from my team is delaying things, I'll crawl back here and apologize," Greg said.

For several hours, Ruth fumed. Then she took comfort in the image of Greg crawling humbly into her office. Then, this morning, she looked at her timeline again. And again.

She had made a mistake! She'd been working from the wrong date. Ruth knew she had to speak to Greg, but she didn't know how to communicate honestly and still save face.

Just go tell him, one part of her urged.

Write it down first, another part said. *That way you won't stumble or get upset.*

Admit the mistake but try to blame it on someone else, another part of her suggested.

Her indecision was making her crazy. Helen, who was often an excellent mentor, was too swamped. She'd worked with Tina before—maybe Tina had some ideas.

Tina listened empathetically. "I hate to make mistakes, too," she said. "I think it's fine to admit to Greg that you were wrong."

Ruth worried that she could appear weak, and Tina advised her to write down what she was going to say and practice it, so she'd feel comfortable. Tina also suggested she talk to Greg soon.

Ruth's heart was racing when she walked into Greg's office. She asked if he had a moment and he nodded, not looking up from his computer.

"Greg, I was wrong," Ruth said slowly. He looked up. "I made a mistake on the timeline—I had written down the wrong date. I didn't realize the error until you mentioned the delay yesterday. When I reviewed the documents, I realized you were right. It's my fault the project is delayed. I apologize. I'd like to brainstorm ways I can help make up the lost time."

Greg smiled and thanked Ruth for her honesty. They looked over the timeline and found a way to make up one day. Greg admitted that being only four days late probably wouldn't hurt anything. Ruth left feeling good about the way she had communicated.

Nobody likes to be wrong. But being honest about your mistakes is one of the more courageous communications you can make. People forget the error and remember the heartfelt apology.

To make a good apology, know who you're talking to. Try to mirror their communication style. Some of the components of an effective apology include:

- Admitting you made a mistake
- Acknowledging the error in a timely manner
- Telling why you made the error
- Offering to make amends

Easing the Pressure Points

Most of us have areas where we're comfortable ad-libbing and other areas where we freeze without preparation. To learn more about your own abilities to communicate under pressure, answer the following questions. Circle any answers that are true for you.

1. I can speak spontaneously in the following kinds of situations:
   - One-on-one
   - A group of colleagues
   - A group of strangers
   - Never. I always like to be prepared.

2. I'm comfortable admitting I don't know something:

- When it's people I know and trust
- When it's an area I don't particularly have expertise in
- Always
- Never

3. I tend to freeze up in the following situations:

- When I'm put on the spot
- When everyone seems to be staring at me or judging me
- Any time I'm speaking out
- I never freeze up

4. When I'm surprised by an unexpected demand or hostile question, I tend to:

- Start talking and hope I think of the right thing to say
- Give myself time to get centered and think about what I want to reply
- Turn the question over to someone else
- Feel furious that the person is attacking me

5. I'd like to improve in these areas of pressure-oriented communication (List areas such as Q and A's in meetings, being called on in a group):

- _____
- _____
- _____
- _____

Review your answers and notice your strengths and challenges. If you're always comfortable communicating on the spot, ask some trusted colleagues for ideas as to how you could be even better. If you are rarely comfortable with speaking spontaneously, consider joining a speaking club such as Toastmasters or asking a confident colleague for some coaching.

Turning Uncertainty Into Confidence

Tina felt more comfortable when she realized it was fine to freeze up and not know an answer. Next time, she decided to let go of any discomfort and invite other people into the question.

It's easier to take the heat when you have your own **HEATING** system:

- **H**onesty
- **E**mpathy
- **A**cknowledgment
- **T**ime frame
- **I**nformation
- **N**ext steps
- **G**ratitude

Chapter Six:

Saying No

Now that she was contributing to the weekly meetings and helping other departments manage their e-mail flow, Courtney had become more professional in her communications and more visible within the company. She had also become more in demand.

Someone asked her to design a communications flow chart. Someone else asked her to serve on the newsletter team. Co-workers or administrative staff from other departments frequently e-mailed or called her with questions. Suddenly she was no longer looking forward to new requests; she was dreading them.

"I'm flattered people are asking me to contribute, but I feel overwhelmed," Courtney told Tina one day at lunch. "But I worry if I don't say yes, people will stop asking me and I'll fade into obscurity again. What should I do?"

Tina was facing her own time crisis. She had a demanding boss and a large workload. She felt like she was constantly behind at work, and she wasn't sure she was using her time wisely. Once, she had not minded working overtime, but now she wanted more time to pursue her own career goals.

Tina suggested they each make a list of the career and professional activities that were most important to them. They could then use these priorities to guide them in saying yes or no to opportunities. They could create a separate list for family, relationship, spiritual, philanthropic and other personal priorities.

Say Yes to Yourself First

Tina started with these questions:

1. What is important to me, career-wise?

2. What career-oriented activities do I do best and most enjoy?

3. How do I currently spend my time?

4. Which of my tasks could someone else do just as well?

5. How can I start shaping my time to meet my goals?

These were her answers:

1. What is important to me, career-wise?

I want to spend more time organizing my techniques for adding creativity to technical writing. I want to write several articles and speeches and give more presentations on the subject. I want to put together my own e-letter and become more visible.

2. What career-oriented activities do I do best and most enjoy?

I like helping people and am good at analyzing situations and relationships. But I'm more interested in expanding my creative writing, public speaking and article writing skills.

3. How do I currently spend my time?

I spend the majority of "extra" time at work advising and counseling people on work-related issues. Part of the advising is related to technical writing, but I feel I'm wasting time sharing the information piecemeal.

4. Which of my tasks could someone else do just as well?

I can think of several people, such as Ruth and Kevin, who could offer support and advice. Some of my overtime is spent proofreading and editing manuals. I'm not good at proofreading, and it takes me ages. Someone like Courtney or Lillian would be better at proofreading.

5. How can I start shaping my time to meet my goals?

I want to say yes to myself and my priorities and a polite no to situations that take me away from my priorities. That includes redirecting people who want work-related or personal advice and saying no to overtime. I plan to:

a. Take two lunch hours a week at my desk, working on writing an article. I will use the contents of this article to send to people who want writing advice (instead of taking so much time talking to them).

b. Send out an e-mail to our technical writing group, telling them I'm looking for speaking opportunities.

c. Ask Ruth and Kevin if they're open to mentoring people.

d. Direct the people who always come to me with their problems to Ruth and Kevin.

e. Say a firm no to overtime.

Know Your Yeses

Think about your own career and answer these questions for yourself.

1. What is important to me career-wise? (Think about how you most want to spend your time.)

   _____

   _____

2. What career-oriented activities do I do best and most enjoy? (If you're uncertain about your skills and talents, ask a couple of co-workers or friends for input.)

   _____

   _____

3. How do I currently spend my time? (If you have any doubts about where your time goes, keep a time log for a day.)

   _____

   _____

4. Which of my tasks could someone else do just as well? (Think about things that are not on your list of priorities or in your area of expertise.)

   _____

   _____

5. How can I start shaping my time to meet my goals? (Be as specific as possible.)

   _____

   _____

The No-What System

"I can't believe after all that goal setting, I just agreed to work overtime this weekend," Courtney told Tina late one afternoon. "It's not even part of my job. Can you help me figure out how to say no next time?"

"Right now, I'm trying to figure out my own boundaries," Tina said. "I think Ruth would be the perfect person to help you power up your no's. Tell her I suggested you contact her."

Tina was honoring her own priorities by saying yes to herself and no to situations that didn't further her goals. She also was trying out her new **No-What** system, an easy method of helping her decide when and how she wanted or needed to say no.

No-What included:

- **What are my options?** Is this a command from a boss, or do I have the option of saying no?

- **What are the potential benefits of saying yes?** These could include: Working in your priority field, visibility, fun or working with new people you want to connect with.

- **What are the challenges or negative byproducts of saying yes?** Try to calculate how much time you'll spend and any risks involved, such as a project that might not be successful or a team that's difficult to work with.

- **What are the negative byproducts of saying no?** Are there any political or personal ramifications? Are you risking a raise, some praise or anything else?

- **What do I gain by saying no?** Examples could include: Time, the joy of setting a boundary or practicing communications skills.

- **What can I say besides yes or no?** Consider your options.

- **What is the most effective way for me to say no?** How do you actually say no to people?

- **What do I feel like after I say no?** Close your eyes and imagine a year has passed. Imagine you said yes—how do you feel? What did you gain? Imagine you said no—how do you feel? What did you gain?

When Tina thought about Courtney's request for additional help, she knew she would have no negative backlash from a refusal and she would get only the smallest positive gain from helping Courtney.

Still, she softened her "no" by offering an option: Ruth would benefit from sharing her techniques with Courtney, and Courtney would benefit from working with someone else.

What Do You "No"?

Apply the **No-What** system to your own life. First think of a time you recently answered with a reluctant yes. Use the system to help you analyze the effectiveness of that yes.

- What were my options? Was this a command from a boss, or did I have the option of saying no?

_____

_____

- What were the potential benefits of saying yes?

_____

_____

- What were the challenges or negative byproducts of saying yes?

_____

_____

- What were the negative byproducts of saying no?

_____

_____

- What did I gain by saying yes?

_____

_____

- What could I have said besides yes?

_____

_____

Now think of a situation when you want to say no. Use the system to help you analyze the effects of saying no.

- What are my options? Is this a command from a boss, or do I have the option of saying no?

_____

_____

- What are the potential benefits of saying yes?

_____

_____

- What are the challenges or negative byproducts of saying yes?

_____

_____

- What are the negative byproducts of saying no?

_____

_____

- What do I gain by saying no?

_____

_____

- What can I say besides yes or no?

  _____

  _____

- What is the most effective way for me to say no? (How do you actually say no to people?)

  _____

  _____

- What do I feel after I say no? (Close your eyes and imagine a year has passed. Imagine you said yes—how do you feel? What did you gain? Imagine you said no—how do you feel? What did you gain?)

  _____

  _____

The Diplomat's Guide to Saying No

There are as many ways to say no as there are types of people who have trouble saying it. Here are some ways to make your no's count.

The People Pleaser's No

Kevin hated to say no. That was one reason he felt constantly overwhelmed. His boss had talked to him about managing his time better; so had his wife. "You have to learn to say no," his friend Stephanie told him.

"I'm a pushover," Kevin said. "I try to say no, I want to say no, but instead I ask questions and listen to the whole story. Then I feel sorry for the person and say yes. I wish I could act differently."

"You can," Stephanie told him. Stephanie was herself a recovering people pleaser and she had spent many hours trapped at meetings, overtime and events because she could not say no.

"I had to learn to pause before I could learn to say no. This **TRADES** idea gives you a chance to think things through before answering," Stephanie said. "For the people pleaser, not having to answer on the spot can make a huge difference."

- **Thank** them for thinking of you
- **Repeat** what they are asking, to make sure you understand their request
- **Assure** them you'll think it over
- **Detach** from the conversation
- **Evaluate** the idea, using the **No-What** system. Take your time. If you're hesitating, ask for support.
- **Say** no in a diplomatic way, offering a simple explanation and appropriate options when possible

The "Ask Me Another Time" No

Ruth really wanted to take the new training her manager offered her, but she knew it wasn't exactly on her priority list. And the timing would eat into her volunteer time.

She wanted to say no for this time, while still showing her interest.

"Thank you for thinking of me. Ordinarily, this is the sort of training I would love to take, but this month I'm all booked up on Wednesdays. I hope you'll consider me for the next class."

Or …

"That sounds like a great opportunity. I can't accept now, but I hope to join you in the future."

The "Other Options" No

Kevin liked the idea of representing his company as part of the City Recycling Center's Advisory Board, but he didn't know if he had the knowledge base or the time. He proposed another option.

> "I'm interested in greening the workplace, but I don't think I have the expertise to serve on this board. How else could I be of service?"

Or ...

> "I'm interested in what this board is doing. However, we're just starting our own recycling program at work, which is a huge time commitment. What if I shared the position with another person?"

The "Networking" No

Tina never liked to turn Helen down. But when Helen asked Tina to take over the newsletter for a month, Tina knew she could not oblige. Still, she wanted to help Helen get the job done, so she offered a Networking No.

> "Thank you for thinking of me. I recommend you contact Ruth. She's looking for an opportunity like this. She'd be excellent."

Or ...

> "I'm flattered you thought of me. I'm not the best person for this particular job, but I know two people who could be quite helpful. Let me send you their contact information."

The "I'm Doing It This Time but Not Again" No

Courtney feared there was no way out of working late. But she didn't want to do it again. She wanted her "no" to reflect how generous she was, not how miserable and upset she felt.

"I'm happy to help you out this once, but my schedule won't allow me to do it again."

Or …

"I appreciate you asking me. I can help you for an hour on Saturday, but I'm afraid that's all the time I have."

If her boss asks Courtney to work overtime again, Courtney will simply:

- Listen to her boss's request without interrupting
- Say no clearly and distinctly
- Explain why, as succinctly as possible
- Suggest an alternative, when appropriate

Professional Pointer:

Once you have decided to decline, say your "no" right away.

For example: "I can't head the holiday committee this year. I'm coaching my daughter's soccer league and many of my evenings are committed. I wonder if you've thought of asking Eileen."

The "Get Me out of Here Now" No

Steve was trapped in one of those endless conversations with a person for whom listening was a foreign language.

A vendor had dropped in and had been talking nonstop for ten minutes about a new product. Steve needed to take action.

"I appreciate the information, but I need to get back to work," Steve said, turning back to the computer.

Or …

"Right now, I need to continue my work," Steve said, standing up and waiting for the vendor to stand. He walked him to the door. "Feel free to send me an e-mail with additional information."

Professional Pointer:

Body language can help emphasize your "no."

The Mythology of Yes

You have to say yes to opportunity … You have to contribute and pitch in … If you're not there for people, they won't be there for you … People get mad at you if you don't help them.

These were some of the "no myths" that raced around in Courtney's head. Yet she saw how the big boss, Helen, said no all the time, and no one seemed angry. Courtney figured there was something powerful about learning to say no.

She was right. Her first no made her feel strong, professional and decisive. She handled herself with poise, offering a "networking no" that connected her boss with a graphic artist in another department.

Her second no, an "ask me again later no," made her smile. Courtney realized when she said no to things that were not her priorities, she was saying yes to herself.

Say Yes With No-Whats

- What are my options?
- What are the potential benefits of saying yes?
- What are the challenges or negative byproducts of saying yes?
- What are the negative byproducts of saying no?
- What do I gain by saying no?
- What can I say besides yes or no?
- What is the most effective way for me to say no?
- What do I feel like after I say no?

Chapter Seven:

Delivering Bad News

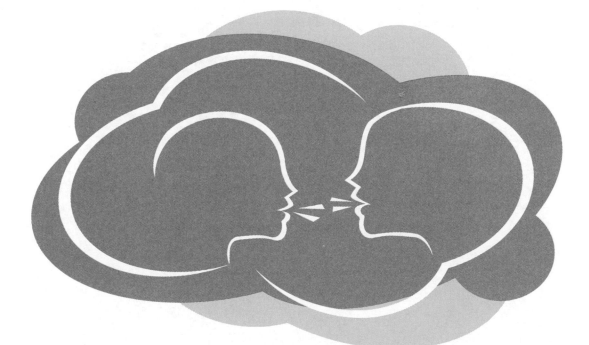

Helen had experienced her fill of delivering bad news. First, the merger. Now, even though the merger had fallen through, budget cuts were looming. She was not looking forward to telling Fred, one of her key managers, that his department was going to have less money and fewer resources.

Helen remembered her great aunt Sally. Sally always was the bearer of bad news. Whenever Sally called, Helen knew something rotten had happened. Helen worried that people would start thinking of her that way—always the bearer of bad news. But for now, that was her job: To do a good job delivering bad news.

Professional Pointer:

Bad news usually doesn't go away, and it doesn't usually improve with age. In fact, the longer you put off discussing the situation, the worse the bad news can seem.

The Savvy SOLDIER

The first time she ever delivered bad news at work, Helen did not prepare. She received a directive from her manager to fire the department's administrative assistant, Gail, whose consistent tardiness and idleness Helen had documented. Helen had spent hours counseling Gail, then giving her warning notices. But the thought of firing her was unnerving. Afraid she would chicken out, Helen just marched into Gail's cubicle and mumbled, "I know you've been wanting to find other work. This is your chance. Your services here are redundant."

Helen left without giving Gail a chance to ask any questions. When Helen returned, Gail was still sitting at her desk, looking puzzled.

"You want to help me find a better job?" Gail asked. "Cool. That's cool."

Helen then had to sit down and redeliver the bad news, this time actually saying, "I have to let you go." Gail cried, ranted and finally packed up her things. From that experience, Helen learned a lot about sharing difficult news with people.

To prepare for the budget cut information, she used the **SOLDIER** technique, to help assure she delivered the news compassionately and clearly:

- **S**elect the right time and place
- **O**utline what you want to say
- **L**ook for something good in the situation
- **D**escribe the situation clearly and concisely
- **I**nclude time for questions and check for understanding
- **E**ngineer and agree on a solution
- **R**equest a follow-up summary or meeting

Tact Tip:

Help the recipient of bad news feel less defensive. Focus on "I" statements rather than "You" statements when you speak.

Envision people's potential responses. Try to prepare answers or information that can help allay further fears or concerns.

Bad News Bearing

Fred was brilliant, decisive and analytical when it came to numbers and systems. When it came to people, he was more hesitant. He worked diligently and sometimes had a hard time holding in his anger. Here's how Helen used **SOLDIER** to guide her conversation with Fred about his department's budget cut.

S—Select the Right Time and Place

Helen selected a conference room where they would not be disturbed by the telephone or other people wandering in. She chose a late afternoon meeting time, right before Fred was scheduled to go home, so that Fred could have a chance to analyze the information and let it sink in without instantly having to go into a meeting or telephone conference.

O—Outline What You Want to Say

Helen outlined the key points. When it came to the specifics of the budget cut, she made more detailed notes. She did not want to omit any important information. This was an executive decision, and she also did not want to criticize or comment on the top leadership's decision.

L—Look for Something Good in the Situation

Helen thought about the old jokes that included the line: There's good news and bad news. Before she delivered the bad news, she tried to think of the good news. She planned to say: "For months, you've been saying you wanted to find the time to analyze operations and see how you could streamline your department. Well, you will now have the time to do that."

D—Describe the Situation Clearly and Concisely

She asked Fred to listen fully before he asked any questions. She figured that would give him a chance to manage his reactions. She detailed the issues, focusing on the problem, not the people. She mentioned the changing market, the rising competition and other factors that had particularly impacted Fred's department. Helen spoke clearly and calmly. She maintained steady eye contact. Even though she felt a little nervous, she truthfully stated the situation without hedging or skirting any issues. She was compassionate but not emotional.

I—Include Time for Questions and Check for Understanding

When she had completed the explanation, she invited questions. She answered each question. She then asked Fred to repeat back his understanding of the budget cut. As he did, she clarified his few misperceptions. By the time they finished the conversation, Helen felt Fred clearly understood the situation.

E—Engineer and Agree on a Solution

Fred was already thinking of how this would affect his operations and his people. They discussed options. Helen wanted to avoid firing anyone if possible. She knew there were openings in other departments and suggested the possibility of transferring people. Knowing that Fred found personnel issues challenging, Helen also volunteered to deliver the bad news to Fred's department.

R—Request a Follow-up Summary or Meeting

The cut would take several months to implement. Fred scheduled a department meeting, so Helen could explain the situation to his staff. Helen scheduled another problem-solving meeting with Fred, so she could hear his recommendations on how they could best implement the cuts.

Hearing and Delivering the Bad News

Most of us have had to hear bad news. Think of a situation where someone has given you bad news. Then answer these questions:

1. What was the person's manner (compassionate, indifferent, emotional, controlled, etc.)?

   _____

   _____

2. How did he or she prepare you for the news?

   _____

   _____

3. What happened after you listened to the news?

   _____

   _____

4. What do you remember most about the conversation?

   _____

   _____

5. What did you appreciate about the way the person delivered the news?

   _____

   _____

6. What do you wish had been different?

   _____

   _____

Now, think of a time when you had to deliver bad news.

1. How did you feel about having to deliver bad news (afraid, nervous, angry, etc.)?

_____

_____

2. What was your manner (compassionate, indifferent, emotional, controlled, etc.)?

_____

_____

3. How did you prepare the person for the news?

_____

_____

4. What happened after he or she listened to the news?

_____

_____

5. What do you remember most about the conversation?

_____

_____

6. What did you like about the way you handled the situation?

_____

_____

7. What do you wish you had done differently?

_____

_____

8. What traits or issues got in the way of delivering the bad news in a professional manner (fears, indirect communication, lack of preparation, etc.)?

_____

_____

Bad News Blowups

Now that he was facing budget cuts, Fred had to counsel one of his employees who was showing up consistently late and doing shoddy work. For weeks, he had been fuming about this, but he had not formally sat down to talk to her. He knew she was an emotional person, and he dreaded the conversation.

Fred went through the scenario in his mind. He wanted to be specific and nonjudgmental. But when he saw Cathy, all his unspoken irritation welled up and he said, "Cathy, for months I've been concerned about the quality of your work and your persistent tardiness."

Before he could finish, Cathy burst into tears and said, "Why didn't you say something? I had no idea. You don't know what I've been going through. You don't know how hard I try to show up at work and do what I can."

Fred was taken aback. He did not know what she was going through. He had never thought to ask why she was showing up late.

"Are there issues you need to discuss with HR?" he asked. He looked at his watch. He had scheduled 15 minutes for this meeting, and he could see she would need more time. Now, he was going to be late for his next meeting. His office phone rang. He did not answer it, but the continuing noise was jarring. Cathy took out another tissue.

"This is so unfair," Cathy said.

The opening bars of "Born to Be Wild" filled the room. Fred had forgotten to turn off his cell phone. He realized he hadn't even delivered the bad news, telling Cathy her work would need to improve. He also realized Cathy wouldn't be able to pay attention in the state she was in. Suddenly, "The Sound of Music" floated into the room—Cathy's cell phone. "Hi honey," she said, sniffling. "I'm in a meeting. Call you later."

Someone tapped on his office door. His next meeting, arriving early.

"Why don't you pull yourself together and come back in an hour," Fred said. "Then we'll finish our conversation."

Cathy left, his next appointment came in, and Fred wished he had thought through the Cathy situation far more carefully.

Fred's experience illustrates what happens when you enter the fray without even a flak jacket instead of being prepared and **SOLDIER**ing through. Fred's experience also illustrates the power of delivering bad news in a timely manner and an appropriate setting.

Professional Pointer:

Since you can't always predict how a person will take difficult news, it's wise to allow the time and space for emotional reactions or lengthy questions.

Make a list of things Fred could have done to improve this meeting. For example, select a private meeting place.

1._____

2._____

3._____

4._____

Professional Pointer:

When people have an emotional reaction, let them express their feelings, but don't let those emotions sway you.

Being Your Own Delivery Service

Ruth was going to miss a deadline due to circumstances outside her control. She decided to deliver the news in advance, so she could keep the situation as positive as possible.

In addition to using the **SOLDIER** technique, she also tried to anticipate her boss's response, so she could counter it in advance. She figured Helen would be disappointed and concerned that the company would lose face and standing with the client.

As they started the meeting, Ruth immediately said, "I've just learned we're going to be a week late with the Kran project. I know this is bad news, and I'm sorry to upset you by having to report it. Here's why we're going to be late. One of the suppliers didn't make the grade, quality-wise. I had to find another supplier. I realize the client may be initially upset, but I think they'll soon see the benefits. The very fact that we're vigilant about the quality of the product should make them understand what a valuable service we're performing for them."

"This is upsetting news," Helen said, but she didn't sound angry. "Let's figure out how we're going to handle this."

By anticipating Helen's reactions, Ruth deflected potential anger and set up a collaborative situation. Knowing what a precise communicator Helen was, Ruth tried to be the same. She kept good eye contact and described the situation as succinctly as possible. She wanted to explain but not blame.

Tact Tip:

When someone does not receive a contract and you have to deliver the bad news via a letter, thank her for her efforts, tell her clearly and succinctly why she did not receive the contract and then thank her again.

Here's an example: "Thank you for meeting with us and for describing the impressive array of your company's services. Though we can see a benefit to working with you, our board has recommended we not switch vendors at this time. We appreciate your time and look forward to our next connection."

The Bad News Barometer

This work won't do … This contact is ending … This benefit is cancelled.

To reduce the emotional reaction many of us have when it comes to delivering bad news, use the **SOLIDER** system to poise yourself for professional and diplomatic communications.

- **<u>S</u>elect** the right time and place
- **<u>O</u>utline** what you want to say
- **<u>L</u>ook** for something good in the situation
- **<u>D</u>escribe** the situation clearly and concisely
- **<u>I</u>nclude** time for questions and check for understanding
- **<u>E</u>ngineer** and agree on a solution
- **<u>R</u>equest** a follow-up summary or meeting

Chapter Eight:

Engendering Appreciation, Praise and Support

"You won't believe what happened," Courtney told Tina when she saw her in the break room. "I was selected to attend this special course on managing e-mails in Washington, D.C. I'm so excited!"

"That's wonderful. You've really worked hard in that area," Tina said. "When do you go?"

Courtney shared the details, then gave Tina a big hug. "Thanks for being so interested," she said. "People are sometimes funny when you tell them something good. Not everyone can celebrate with you. And I want to celebrate."

Tina remembered when Ruth had encouraged her to send her good news to the company newsletter. She e-mailed Courtney with that suggestion. As she wrote, she thought about the power of sharing and celebrating good news, making the most of opportunities and giving people the praise they deserved. To help her remember these simple components, Tina created **SNAP**:

- **Share** your own good news
- **Notice** others' accomplishments
- **Accept** opportunities that increase your chances for praise and visibility
- **Praise** when you can

Tina decided to add more **SNAP** to her communications.

S—Share Your Own Good News

Tina thought about the light in Courtney's eyes as she shared the news of her training. Tina had felt encouraged by hearing how Courtney's hard work, helping so many people with their e-mail issues, had paid off.

Thinking about Courtney's good news made Tina think about the presentation she was giving in two weeks, a talk on adding creativity to technical manuals.

A woman from Tina's tech writers' group was hosting a lunch-and-learn event at her company. "You're welcome to invite people," her hostess had said.

Inspired by Courtney, Tina decided to send the news about her presentation to her growing e-mail list. She would also send individual e-mails to her department heads.

Her goals were to:

- Keep herself visible
- Remind people of her expertise in creative technical writing
- Increase support from her department heads
- Invite people to the presentation
- Inspire others to share their expertise and their good news

As Tina worked on her e-mail, she tried to stick with the facts. She didn't want her good news to come across as bragging.

Tact Tip:

Target your good news to fit your audience. With your friends, you can praise yourself and be excited and overjoyed. When you tell or e-mail colleagues and other business associates, focus on the facts and the benefits to others. That professional focus reduces the risk of seeming egotistical.

Meanwhile, Kevin was struggling with some good news. He had just been chosen to write a semimonthly column on greening up the workplace for the local newspaper. His friend Ed had applied to write the same column, but had not been chosen. Kevin's elation was dampened by the prospect of telling Ed. He wanted to be both sensitive and truthful and didn't know exactly how or what to say.

Tact Tip:

When your good news is a friend's bad news, think through how you want to communicate it. When possible, tell the friend before you share the news with others. If there's an element of luck in you being chosen, focus on that. This is also a good time to notice and appreciate the friend or colleague's accomplishments, if you can do so sincerely.

Share your own good news

Think of some good news you'd like to share. Answer these questions:

- What are my goals in sharing this news?

  1. _____

  2. _____

  3. _____

- What are the best ways to share the news?

  1. _____

  2. _____

  3. _____

- Who do I most want to share this news with?

  1. _____

  2. _____

  3. _____

- Is there anyone who will feel awkward or uncomfortable hearing this news? If so, how shall I communicate with him or her?

  1. _____

  2. _____

  3. _____

N—Notice Others' Accomplishments

Tina had felt encouraged and happy when Steve noticed her accomplishments regarding the technical writers' group. His words of praise made her look for ways she could do even more. She also felt affirmed and acknowledged. Tina decided to be more vigilant in observing and then appreciating the interesting things people were doing.

Tina made a list of some ways she could learn more about the accomplishments of others. Her list included:

- Reading the company newsletter
- Asking people open-ended questions, such as "What's making you happy these days?"
- Noticing new innovations at work and asking, "Whose idea was this?"
- Keeping up with local events

She also thought about the best ways to appreciate the accomplishments. For some, an e-mail or voicemail would be enough. For others, she bought some blank cards so she could write a quick personal note. Most people saw those greeting cards as something special, and Tina knew how she enjoyed the cards people occasionally sent her.

Noticing others' accomplishments

Noticing and affirming people is one easy way to be a memorable communicator.

- What are some ways you can increase your awareness of others' accomplishments?

  1. _____

  2. _____

  3. _____

- What are some easy ways to acknowledge these accomplishments? When appropriate, be creative.

  1. _____

  2. _____

  3. _____

A—Accept Opportunities That Increase Your Chances for Praise and Visibility

Courtney had taken the opportunity to help people manage their e-mail and had received a lot of praise and visibility. Plus she felt more confident and professional.

Tina had taken the opportunity to give a presentation to her writing group and had received lots of positive feedback and other opportunities.

Tina saw how sharing ideas and talents inspired praise, created visibility and often led to more opportunities.

Though she had vowed not to work overtime, she decided to look for chances to speak or write articles, two areas she was quite passionate about. She also decided to look for opportunities that were right for others. Her opportunity alert included:

- Revving up her listening skills, being alert for needs and opportunities
- Learning more about the types of opportunities others were seeking. Her "noticing" skills helped her with this.
- Asking questions when she heard of potential opportunities, so she could share information with others

Professional Pointer:

Help others connect to opportunities. People will appreciate your thoughtfulness when you notice ways they can share their talents and abilities.

P—Praise When You Can

Tina remembered the first time her team leader had said "Good job." Those words had made her feel acknowledged and smart. That praise made her think more highly of the team leader. When he next asked her to do something, she agreed enthusiastically.

She thought of how Jane's face had brightened when Tina praised her on getting her project turned in two days early.

These were both everyday events, but the words of acknowledgement made a big difference.

Tina wanted to be the kind of communicator who appreciated people. She decided to be more diligent in noticing and praising the work that people were doing.

She also vowed to praise and thank the people who helped her. Steve had helped her develop her presentation skills. Courtney had listened to her practice. She wanted to praise and thank these people.

Tina remembered when Helen had praised her for creating a readable format for a computer manual. That specific praise pleased her and also let her know exactly what Helen was appreciating. Helen's praise inspired Tina to explore ways to make the next manual even more readable.

Tina knew she would see Courtney in the break room. When she did, she said, "I never did properly thank you for coaching me on my presentation. You were so patient to listen to that speech so many times, and each time, you had a valuable piece of information that made it stronger. I really appreciate all your help."

Courtney's face lit up. "Thank you. I didn't really know if my ideas were useful, but I'm glad I was able to help."

Tina saw the effect of sincere and specific praise, and she vowed to be more diligent in thanking people for their help and praising them for their accomplishments.

Professional Pointer:

When appropriate, give people public praise and recognition for their accomplishments.

Tact Tip:

When you're praising or acknowledging people, use an enthusiastic tone and gestures.

Your Own SNAP Shots

Look for **SNAP**py ways you can:

- **Share** your own good news
- **Notice** others' accomplishments
- **Accept** opportunities that increase your chances for praise and visibility
- **Praise** when you can

Chapter Nine:
Leading With Language

"It's nice to see you taking a larger leadership role in the organization," Steve said to Tina at one of their planning sessions for the technical writers' group.

"Thanks, but I haven't really been doing anything differently," Tina said. She thought of herself as a diligent worker, but she rarely considered herself a leader. Still, she felt a little inward glow at Steve's compliment.

"You may not realize what a role model you've become," Steve told her. "First, you gave your presentation. Then you organized the panel, so we could all share tips. You've asked people for ideas for your newsletter. And you've been a clear and constant communicator about the goals of our group. I call that leadership."

Tina had always equated leadership with someone in a high ranking management position. Tina did not have such a position. But Steve's observations expanded her views and made her wonder: How can I be more of a leader, both within the tech writers' group and at work?

"Why do you want to be more of a leader?" Courtney asked her several days later, when Tina was discussing the issue. "That seems like so much work, always being available to people, taking criticism for decisions and being responsible when things go wrong. I'm happy the way I am."

"I don't want to work harder or move into more of a management position," Tina said. "I'm not looking for more power or decision-making responsibilities. I'd like to be the sort of low-key leader who can influence, inspire and motivate people."

Tina wanted to approach leadership in a way that made sense for her. So she asked herself a few questions:

1. What does leadership mean to me? Who are some leaders I admire?

2. What are my goals in wanting to assume more leadership?

3. What situations and environments bring out the leader in me? How can I show more leadership in those areas?

4. Are there situations or environments where I shrink from leadership? Why am I uncomfortable in these situations?

5. Are there areas where I'd like to be more prominent? How can I show more leadership in those areas?

6. Who can help or encourage me?

7. Who else will benefit from my increased leadership? Are there ways I can work with or collaborate with the other beneficiaries?

Over the next weeks, Tina jotted down answers to these questions. Just writing down her thoughts helped her clarify her goals.

1. What does leadership mean to me? Who are the leaders I admire?

Tina instantly thought of her department head, Helen. Helen was always kind, complimentary and open to new ideas. She was an excellent conversationalist, asking questions and listening attentively to the answers. She was open to new ideas. Helen was also decisive, but she seemed compassionate as well.

Tina realized leadership meant influencing, motivating and inspiring others. That meant building relationships and deepening trust levels. Helen seemed to embody those skills, and Tina could see herself incorporating some of Helen's leadership traits.

2. What are my goals in wanting to assume more leadership?

Tina's goals included:

- Becoming more visible at work and in her professional organization
- Improving her conversational, communication, presentation and written skills
- Inspiring and motivating others in her profession and her workplace

3. What situations and environments bring out the leader in me? How can I show more leadership in those areas?

Tina felt most comfortable one-on-one or in small groups where people already knew and liked her. This included her tech writers' group. According to Steve, Tina was using her leadership abilities in that group. She could show more leadership in that organization by:

- Offering an inspiring quote or tip at each meeting. (This would strengthen her speaking skills and allow her to offer inspiration.)

- Sending members a congratulatory e-mail when she learned of some triumph or accomplishment. (This would encourage others, build trust and heighten her writing skills.)

- Noticing the gifts and talents of members and sharing her observations with the member and others. (This would encourage others, build trust, improve listening and conversational skills and create an atmosphere of appreciation.)

- Working to get people more involved and thus more appreciated. (This would encourage her to deepen her listening skills and use her influencing and communications skills.)

4. Are there situations or environments where I shrink from leadership? Why am I uncomfortable in these situations?

Tina did often feel uncomfortable in work meetings or even in giving out assignments as the team leader. As she wrote this list, she realized that she didn't feel bonded with her co-workers. They were always under deadline and in a hurry. She wasn't sure they liked her, and she wasn't sure how much she liked them.

5. Are there other areas where I'd like to be more prominent? How can I show more leadership in those areas?

Tina knew she could be more prominent at work. She had often led team projects, but everyone in her work group was fairly self-sufficient. She usually just assigned tasks, and the team members usually turned in their work on time. When someone was late, she e-mailed them a reminder or left them a voice message, avoiding potential conflict. Tina realized she could be a more effective leader by:

- Inviting more input and ideas from others. (This would strengthen her listening and conversational skills and improve her ability to ask open-ended questions.)

- Noticing when someone did outstanding work and complimenting him or her. (This would improve her listening and communication skills, empower others and build confidence and trust. She would also be role modeling.)

- Having a small celebration when they all successfully reached a deadline. (This could involve and motivate others, offer opportunities for conversations and connections and increase her comfort level.)

6. Who can help or encourage me?

Steve had already encouraged her. Tina decided to share her ideas with Steve and get his input. Courtney was always encouraging. Tina also decided to talk with Helen and see if she would be willing to mentor her. She thought of several writers in her group who were already leading large work teams. They might be willing to share information and ideas.

7. Who else will benefit from my increased leadership? Are there ways I can work with or collaborate with the other beneficiaries?

Tina felt everyone in her department and in the writers' group could possibly benefit. She decided to ask Helen about training opportunities in the fields of leadership and communication.

Understanding Your Inner Leader

Consider your own leadership goals and opportunities as you answer these questions.

1. What does leadership mean to me? Who are some leaders I admire?

2. What are my goals in wanting to assume more leadership?

3. What situations and environments bring out the leader in me? How can I show more leadership in those areas?

4. Are there situations or environments where I shrink from leadership? Why am I uncomfortable in these situations?

5. Are there areas where I'd like to be more prominent? How can I show more leadership in those areas?

6. Who can help or encourage me?

7. Who else will benefit from my increased leadership? Are there ways I can work with or collaborate with the other beneficiaries?

Transforming Goals Into Words and Actions

Even though she thought of herself as a people person, Tina was also a "get things done now" person. She often just e-mailed her team their tasks without asking for input or ideas. Now that she was working on leadership skills, she realized she needed to practice the art of conversation and include language that was more motivating and involving.

Here was one of her first attempts when the team of four writers crowded around her desk in her office.

"We have a new project deadline next Wednesday. Each of you has a folder with your assignment. Take a look and let me know what you think."

"I'll have my part done," Jill said, already preparing to leave the room. She sounded irritated and resigned, rather than inspired or motivated.

"Fine," Darren said. He sounded worn out. The others just nodded and filed out of the room without a smile or nod.

Tina sat still, stewing. She'd invited input, "Let me know what you think." But nobody seemed to hear her. She called Steve for advice. Steve offered her some language softeners, designed to invite people into conversation rather than give them information.

He also suggested she ask herself: "How would a true leader respond in this situation?"

Here are Steve's "Speak **SOFT**" suggestions:

> - **Suggest** rather than order or inform
> - **Observe**
> - **Follow** through on what you observe
> - **Try** to engage and involve people

Tina used the **SOFT** template to replay her interaction with the team and see how she might have incorporated more leadership skills into her communications.

S—Suggest Rather Than Order or Inform

Instead of handing everyone a task and deadline, she might have said:

"We have a new project, and I'd really welcome your ideas."

Or …

"I'd like to hear your thoughts on this new project."

O—Observe

Steve advised Tina to capitalize on her abilities to understand and observe people.

Tina was ever-observant and empathetic. She heard the irritation in Jill's voice. She saw Darren's tiredness. She noticed how the other two did not give her eye contact. She herself felt frazzled at the thought of yet another deadline. She saw and felt how discouraged and unappreciated everyone felt, but she had done and said nothing. Yet these were some of the very people she wanted to influence, motivate and inspire.

F—Follow Through on What You Observe

Tina often felt flattered when someone asked her for advice. She liked it when someone valued her opinion.

When she heard Jill's irritation or saw Darren's tiredness, she could have said:

"Jill, you sound concerned. I'd like to hear your thoughts."

Or …

"Darren, you seem tired. Let's talk the project through. Maybe we can come up with a way to divide the work so we don't feel such deadline pressure."

She could have followed through with her team by creating common ground and saying:

"I don't know about you all, but I'm feeling pretty worn down. I wonder what we can do to make these deadlines less daunting. I'd love to hear suggestions from each of you."

Or …

"Before we begin this project, let's do some brainstorming. Maybe together we can make this less stressful."

T—Try to Engage and Involve People

At the tech writers' group or in the break room, Tina usually felt right at home. She got into conversations with people, asked them questions and learned about their work and their lives. Because she always felt so rushed for time, she did not know much about her colleagues. One of the guys, Seth, seemed rather gloomy and unpleasant. He'd been late for deadlines twice, and Tina generally tried to politely avoid him.

Tina thought of ways she could have engaged and involved her team:

- Reserved the conference room and set up a short meeting
- Let people know about the meeting either by dropping into their office or by calling them (Instead, she sent an impersonal group e-mail.)
- Had snacks available
- Started the meeting with some conversation
- Set up a small ritual, sharing either one thing each person had learned that month or one thing each was passionate about outside the workplace
- Included sincere and specific praise for each person, including something she had noticed from earlier projects about their abilities or talents
- Incorporated brainstorming and problem-solving before handing out the assignments

Tact Tip:

Even when you want to communicate directly, you can still soften your style by saying, "I suggest … " or "One way to begin is … "

The Art of Leading Through Dynamic Dialogue

Steve was surprised when he began finding information and articles about the art of dialogue and conversation. "Meaningful conversation can influence others," he read.

"It sounds like conversation is a leadership tool," he told Tina when they next met.

"Then I'm in luck. I love to talk to people."

"I do too. But I notice that more people like to talk and fewer people like to listen. I guess that's where the leadership component kicks in, really listening and then responding to people."

Tina thought of various meetings and social settings she had recently experienced. A meaningful conversation, with equal parts listening and talking, complete with eye contact and undivided attention, was rare. Tina wanted to make more conversational connections with people.

As she observed the communications around her, including her own, she created this **MEANS** test to help her create the foundation for a leading-edge conversation.

- **Manage** your own ego, words and emotions
- **Engage** people by showing interest in them and asking open-ended questions
- **Avoid** interrupting
- **Nurture** your listening skills by giving eye contact and your complete attention
- **Show** your enthusiasm and understanding of what people are saying

Think about your own conversations. Make a list of places and ways you could engineer more meaningful dialogue.

For example, Tina's places might include: The technical writers' group, the break room and her own work group.

Places:

1._____

2._____

3._____

4._____

Tina planned to inspire deeper conversation by sharing something from her life or asking for advice on a meaningful issue, such as the balance between working overtime and earning extra money vs. spending more time with family.

Ways you can inspire meaningful conversation:

1._____

2._____

3._____

4._____

Speaking From the Leading Edge

In this book, you've explored tools and techniques for heightening your communication expertise. The more you communicate with professionalism and diplomacy, the more leadership skills you will develop.

Enjoy the art form of discovering your own personal communication gifts … and share your talents in the workplace.